IF EXTINCT BEA

PREHISTORIC PREDATORS

Thanks to the creative team:
Senior Editor: Alice Peebles
Consultant: Neil Clark
Fact Checker: Kate Mitchell
Design: www.collaborate.agency

Hungry Tomato™
A division of Lerner Publishing Group, Inc.
241 First Avenue North
Minneapolis, MN 55401 USA

For reading levels and more information, look up this title at www.lernerbooks.com.

Main body text set in Franklin Gothic Book 11/12.
Typeface provided by International Typeface Corp.

Library of Congress Cataloging-in-Publication Data

Names: Rake, Matthew. | Mendez, Simon, illustrator.
Title: Prehistoric predators / Matthew Rake ; illustrated by Simon Mendez.
Description: Minneapolis : Hungry Tomato, 2017. | Series: If extinct beasts came to life | Audience: Age 8–12. | Audience: Grade 4 to 6. | Includes index.
Identifiers: LCCN 2016028376 (print) | LCCN 2016029275 (ebook) | ISBN 9781512406337 (lb : alk. paper) | ISBN 9781512411607 (pb : alk. paper) | ISBN 9781512409079 (eb pdf)
Subjects: LCSH: Dinosaurs—Juvenile literature. | Predatory animals—Juvenile literature.
Classification: LCC QE861.5 .R354 2017 (print) | LCC QE861.5 (ebook) | DDC 560—dc23

LC record available at https://lccn.loc.gov/2016028376

Manufactured in the United States of America
1-39306-21143-9/6/2016

IF EXTINCT BEASTS CAME TO LIFE

PREHISTORIC PREDATORS

by Matthew Rake
Illustrated by Simon Mendez

WARNING!
These extinct beasts are not alive today, and the encounters seen in this book are not real. But just imagine if they were . . .

CONTENTS

THE BIG, THE BAD, AND THE UGLY

Everyone knows about the dinosaurs and how scary some of them were. But did you know there were lots of other equally savage prehistoric creatures? How about the crocodile that liked to dine on dinosaurs? Or the bird that stood 8 feet (2.5 meters) tall and used its 18-inch (46 centimeter) beak like a hatchet? Now can you imagine what might happen if they arrived back in today's world? Well, you are about to find out . . .

All life started in the sea—and that's where the first animals evolved, around 550 million years ago. Some were pretty weird, such as 2.5-inch (6 cm) *Opabinia* (*right*) with its five eyes and long grasping claw at the end of a long nose.

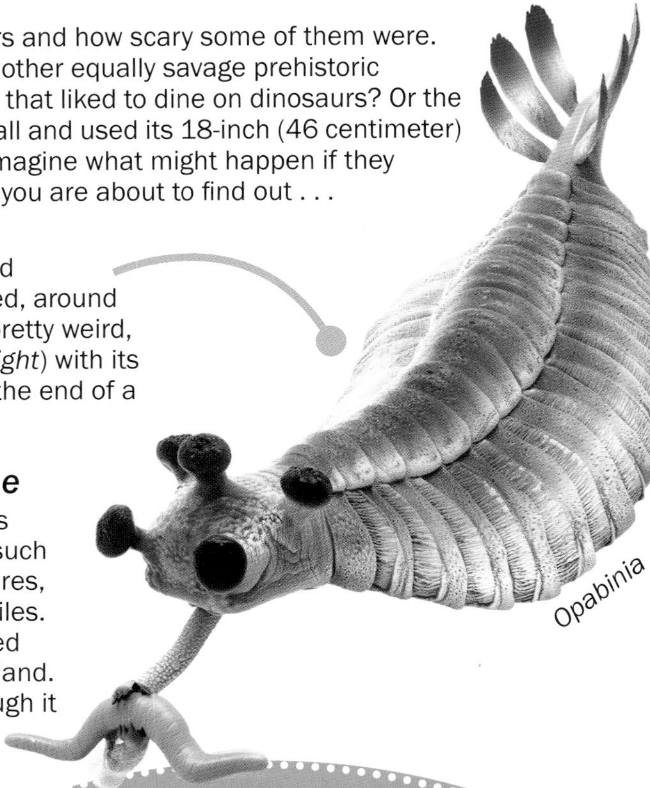

Opabinia

Pretty soon, animals became ferocious. About 475 million years ago, there were massive predators such as sea scorpions and shelled creatures, called nautiloids, as large as crocodiles. Eventually, some sea animals evolved limbs and hauled themselves on to land. One was *Acanthostega* (*below*), though it probably still kept close to water.

Acanthostega

Reptiles were the first animals with backbones to live only on land. Some grew to enormous sizes, like the fearsome *Sarcosuchus* (*see page 12*). Some evolved leathery wings and took to the skies. One of the first flying reptiles, or pterosaurs, was *Eudimorphodon* (*below*). ***The largest was Quetzalcoatlus (see page 14), which hunted or scavenged on land.***

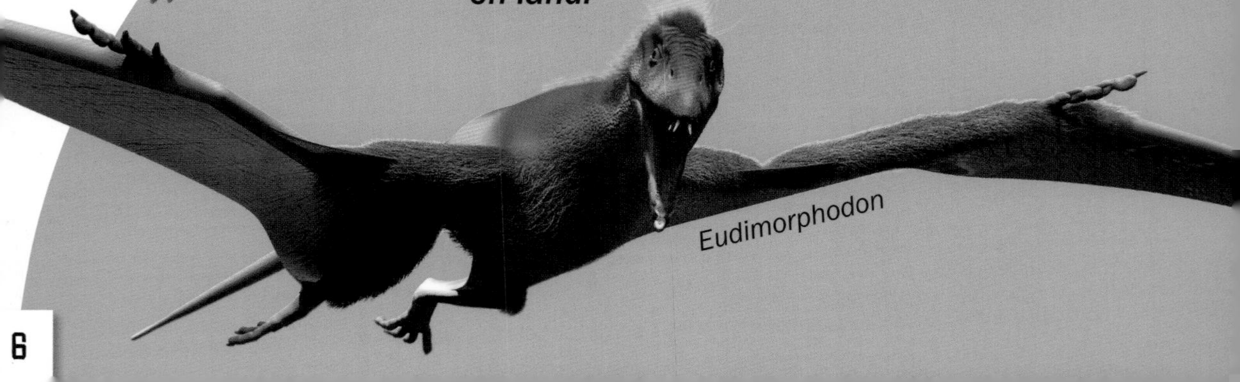

Eudimorphodon

Mammals started evolving at the same time as dinosaurs and pterosaurs, about 230 million years ago or even earlier. Like the first sea creatures, they were mostly very small, but after the dinosaurs died out, ***mammals grew to massive proportions.***

These big mammals were equipped with powerful jaws and muscles that made them very dangerous predators. The saber-toothed cat, *Smilodon* (*left and page 24*), which lived until 10,000 years ago, weighed up to 880 pounds (400 kilograms)—much more than any of today's big cats. ***And birds became gigantic and ferocious too!***

Now you can ***meet mighty Smilodon*** along with terror birds (*see page 22*), killer pigs (*below and page 20*), and brutal reptiles. Imagine if they came back to life to cause carnage and commotion!

If you've got the courage, read on . . . just be prepared for some bizarre and scary encounters between modern animals and prehistoric beasts.

Smilodon

Killer pigs

ROCKING THE BOAT

DIMETRODON

Er, there appears to be a rather unexpected entrant in this year's yacht race. It has a sail, but it doesn't look interested in the race. In fact, it seems to be going after the sailors, not the first prize. This curious creature is *Dimetrodon,* and why it had a sail on its back is a mystery. It was certainly not to help it glide across the water—although that was one of the theories when this reptile-like creature was first discovered in the nineteenth century. Another theory was that it might swim on its back and use the sail like a fin! Other people thought the sail camouflaged the animal among reeds as it waited for prey—though a better way of concealing yourself might be not having one at all!

For this capsized yachtsman, *Dimetrodon*'s sail should be the last thing on his mind—it's the teeth he should be worried about. *Dimetrodon* was one of the first animals to have jagged teeth perfect for slicing through flesh . . .

DIMETRODON

PRONOUNCED
Die-MEH-troe-don

LIVED
North America and Western Europe (one species), 290 million–270 million years ago

LENGTH
About 10 feet (3 m)

WEIGHT
500 pounds (225 kg)

WARMING UP

Experts now think the sail might have controlled *Dimetrodon*'s body temperature. Cold-blooded reptiles need to warm up in the morning, and maybe the sail helped *Dimetrodon* to soak up sunshine. Or perhaps, like the peacock's tail, it was a way of attracting mates—the male *Dimetrodon* did have a bigger sail than the female!

EUROPEAN SPECIES

So far scientists have found thirteen species of *Dimetrodon*. The first one was discovered in 1878. The latest discovery, *Dimetrodon teutonis*, found in 2001 in Germany, is the only species to have been found in Europe.

RUTHLESS REPTILE

INOSTRANCEVIA

Wolves are very territorial—they roam over many miles, defending their range by howling and scent-marking. But more strong-arm tactics will be necessary to tackle this impostor. It's *Inostrancevia*, which had lethal canine teeth up to 6 inches (15 cm) long in its upper jaw. Its back teeth were tiny in comparison, but this didn't matter because *Inostrancevia* didn't chew its food. It simply ripped open prey and swallowed large chunks of meat. Its lower jaw was hinged so it could open its mouth very wide. One of the cubs might be swallowed whole if it really wanted to wolf down its meal.

Inostrancevia lived before the age of the dinosaurs. It was a reptile but belonged to the therapsid group from which mammals evolved. Reptiles generally have sprawling limbs, but *Inostrancevia* had a more upright posture. Compared to other animals of the time, it was a good runner as its legs were long relative to the size of its body. But it is not going to outpace these wolves—they can run for 30 miles (48 kilometers) a day. For this *Inostrancevia*, it's not a question of fight or flight. It's just fight . . .

INOSTRANCEVIA

PRONOUNCED
In-oh-stran-SEE-vee-ah

LIVED
Northern Russia, 260 million–254 million years ago

LENGTH
Up to 11 feet, 6 inches (3.5 m); skull: up to 24 inches (60 cm) long

SPECIAL FEATURES

Inostrancevia is known as a gorgonopsian reptile. This order of reptiles had many mammal-like features, including different-shaped teeth, well-developed ear bones, and upright legs. But they are not thought to have had fur like mammals.

COLD-BLOODED KILLER

SARCOSUCHUS

There has been major disruption on the subway system today. But finally something is emerging from the tunnel. Arriving now on platform 1 is, er... a crocodile. And not just any crocodile. This is *Sarcosuchus*—in the days of the dinosaurs, it used to lie in wait in rivers. And even the deadliest dinos needed to be extra careful. *Sarcosuchus* was the length of a bus, weighed more than an elephant, and had more than 100 teeth, including bone-crushing incisors. And for protection, it was covered head to tail with scutes, hard plates covered with horn. Basically, it had its own personal suit of armor.

It was also a pretty cunning predator. Like today's crocodiles, *Sarcosuchus* probably waited submerged in shallow water, with its eyes just above the water. In this position, it could look around without moving its head. Unsuspecting dinosaurs that came down for a drink would end up as dinner.

So a word of advice for the commuters here: "Stand back from the platform edge—there is a *Sarcosuchus* approaching!"

TOP THAT

The biggest modern crocodile ever measured was Lolong, which lived in captivity in the Philippines. It was 20 feet, 4 inches (6.2 m) long and weighed 1.2 tons (1.1 metric tons). *Sarcosuchus* was about eight times heavier and twice as long.

SARCOSUCHUS

PRONOUNCED

Sark-oh-SUE-kuss

LIVED

Africa and South America, 112 million years ago

LENGTH

39 feet (12 m); skull: 6 feet (1.8 m)

WEIGHT

8.8 tons (8 metric tons)

EPIC FIGHTS?

Sarcosuchus lived in what is now the Sahara in North Africa. Back then, it wasn't a desert but a lush, tropical region with lots of rivers. *Spinosaurus*, the biggest meat-eating dinosaur ever, also lived there. It's likely the two creatures had epic fights together.

SOARING PTEROSAUR

QUETZALCOATLUS

Okay, at a watering hole, you'd expect giraffes. But what about the other creatures? They are *Quetzalcoatlus*, and it looks like they have flown in for a quick feed. They're gobbling up the small lizards, amphibians, and mammals that live near the water.

Quetzalcoatlus was a pterosaur, a type of flying reptile. Pterosaurs evolved 230 million years ago or earlier, about the same time as the dinosaurs. And just like dinosaurs, they got bigger and bigger. *Quetzalcoatlus* lived some 72–66 million years ago and was the biggest pterosaur of all. And if you think it looks big on the ground, imagine it in flight. It is the largest flying creature ever, with a wingspan as wide as a fighter jet.

One thing, however, is a little mystifying: how did this creature get in the air? Some scientists think it jumped from a cliff or used a downward slope as a runway. Others think it vaulted into the air from all fours in what they call a quad jump! If so, these giraffes had better get away before they're knocked out by those giant wings . . .

QUETZALCOATLUS

PRONOUNCED
Kwet-ZAL-co-AT-luss

LIVED
North America,
72 million–66 million years ago

LENGTH
About 33–36 feet
(10–11 m)

WEIGHT
About 440–550 pounds
(200–250 kg)

UP AND AWAY

One study in 2012 found that *Quetzalcoatlus* could fly at 80 miles per hour (130 km/h) for 7 to 10 days at altitudes of 15,000 feet (4,570 m). Its maximum range was probably about 8,000–12,000 miles (12,800–19,000 km).

WALKING WHALE

AMBULOCETUS

Can you imagine an animal that swam like a whale but could also walk on dry land? Well, meet *Ambulocetus*. It's the big-headed animal on the right of the picture here.

On the left, a crocodile has just attacked a wildebeest—it's in the middle of killing it with its death roll. But it might have to endure a death roll of its own from *Ambulocetus*. Looks like a double dish of crocodile and wildebeest today for this prehistoric predator.

So how on earth did the strange-looking *Ambulocetus* come about? Around 50 million years ago, mammals were built for life on solid ground, but some started to evolve into sea creatures. Why? Probably because food was scarce on land and the sea was full of tasty treats: fish and crustaceans such as crabs, lobsters, and crayfish. One of the first to do this was *Ambulocetus*. It could walk on land but was also at home in the water—as this crocodile is about to find out!

AMBULOCETUS

PRONOUNCED
Am-bew-low-SEE-tuss

LIVED
Shores of India, 50 million–48 million years ago

LENGTH
About 10 feet (3 m)

WEIGHT
440–660 pounds (200–300 kg)

GOOD VIBRATIONS

Ambulocetus probably picked up sound vibrations both in and out of the water through its lower jawbone. These sounds passed up to the inner ear. This is how modern predatory whales hear—they have no external part of the ear.

SPEEDY SWIMMER

Ambulocetus swam by arching its spine and pushing its lower body up and down in the water, like an otter or a whale. Powerful kicks with its back legs, which probably had webbed toes, gave the animal extra speed.

BONE CRUNCHER

ANDREWSARCHUS

In Asia, the tiger is the apex predator. This means no other animal preys on it. Big tigers can measure 10 feet (3 m) and have skulls 14 inches (35 cm) long. Well, here the tiger has more than met its match—it's the monster *Andrewsarchus*.

Scientists have only ever found one skull of *Andrewsarchus*, but it is more than double the length of a tiger's. The size of the body is anyone's guess—but if it were in the same proportion as a tiger, it would be more than 26 feet (8 m) long! Scientists don't think it would have reached these lengths—but they are pretty sure it was the largest carnivorous land mammal ever. The size of the cheekbones tell us the jaws would have had tremendously powerful muscles. These muscles, together with its huge teeth, would have been perfect for delivering a fatal bite to the skull of another animal.

So, although they say don't catch a tiger by the tail, this *Andrewsarchus* shouldn't be too worried. After all, he is the apex predator here.

ANDREWSARCHUS

PRONOUNCED
Ann-droo-SAR-kuss

LIVED
Central Asia,
48 million–41 million
years ago

SKULL LENGTH
33 inches (83 cm);
width: 22 inches (56 cm)

DINNER MENU

What did *Andrewsarchus* eat? Some scientists have suggested turtles because the only *Andrewsarchus* fossil to be found was in a prehistoric coastal area. But they could also have eaten giant herbivorous mammals, such as the rhino-like *Brontotherium*.

KILLER PIG

ENTELODONT

You've heard of foxes raiding a chicken shed and dogs chasing sheep in fields. But a pig terrorizing a farm? That couldn't happen, right? Oh yes it could, if the pig in question is an entelodont. They certainly want more than a few roots and grains on their dinner menu.

Entelodonts are often simply referred to as killer pigs. And here's why: they were massive creatures, at least twice the size of today's pigs. Their huge skulls had jaws and muscles designed for bone crushing. Fossils of primitive rhinos and camels have been found with wounds that were made by entelodonts.

They would even attack other entelodonts. Many entelodont skulls have severe gashes up to 0.8 inches (2 cm) deep, which can only have been inflicted by other killer pigs. From studying these wounds, scientists can tell it was common for one pig to have its rival's head entirely in its mouth!

So this rancher should get out of that barn as quickly as possible. And if the entelodont wants to stay the night, let it!

ENTELODONT

PRONOUNCED
en-TELL-oh-dont

LIVED
North America, Europe, and Asia, 37 million–16 million years ago

LENGTH
Up to 11.5 feet (3.5 m)

WEIGHT
About 925 pounds (420 kg)

BIG HEAD

Daeodon was one of the largest entelodonts. It lived about 20 million years ago, and its skull was about 3 feet (0.9 m) long—that's slightly bigger than a standard oil drum!

TERROR BIRD

PHORUSRHACID

This race has an unexpected entrant. Scientists call it a *phorusrhacid,* but as that is tricky to pronounce, it's often called a "terror bird." And you can see why. With a massive head, long, powerful legs, and fearsome talons, the terror bird was a bit like a smaller version of *T. rex.* So you can be sure it has not come along for the ride—it's here for the riders! And chances are that it will get one.

How do we know terror birds were ferocious meat-eaters? One important clue is that their beaks curved downwards into a hook-like tip. Every living bird of prey has a beak like this for tearing off flesh—so it's a clear sign that terror birds also had a taste for meat. Indeed, the terror birds' hooks were so big that scientists think they were used to strike down repeatedly on prey with quick stabbing motions. The beak could be up to 18 inches (46 cm) long and some birds grew 8–10 feet (2.5–3 m) tall—so it would be a bit like someone standing over you, hitting you with a hatchet!

PHORUSRHACID

PRONOUNCED
FOR-uss-RAY-kid

LIVED
South and North America, 60 million–2 million years ago

HEIGHT
Up to about 10 feet (3 m)

WEIGHT
Up to 550 pounds (250 kg)

UP TO SPEED

If you think the bird here would not keep up with the horses, think again. The fastest racehorse ran at 44 miles per hour (71 km/h). Some scientists estimate that *Mesembriornis*, a 5-foot (1.5 m) terror bird, galloped along at 60 miles per hour (97 km/h).

FANGTASTIC FELINE

SMILODON

We all know about the ferocity of modern lions, tigers, and leopards. Well, they are pussycats compared to the saber-toothed cats. These prehistoric predators were generally bigger and more powerfully built—and the largest of all was *Smilodon*. It had powerful front legs and fangtastic canines: they were 8 inches (20 cm) long and jagged on both edges.

Smilodon lived in North and South America and hunted bison and camels, and maybe even baby mammoths and giant sloths. But most of these animals don't live in the wild anymore. So the *Smilodon* in this picture have found other prey: a bear.

How did *Smilodon* capture its prey? There was probably no running involved. *Smilodon* was heavy and had a very short tail, which meant its balance and agility would have been poor, unlike most modern big cats. So scientists think *Smilodon* had to be more cunning—it probably pounced on prey from trees or rocks. Then it would sink its teeth into its victim's neck and wait until the wounded animal bled to death.

SMILODON

PRONOUNCED
SMY-loh-don

LIVED
North and South America, 2 million–10,000 years ago

LENGTH
6 feet (1.8 m)

WEIGHT
Up to 880 pounds (400 kg)

COME TOGETHER

Scientists believe that *Smilodon* lived in packs. Why? Because fossils often show they had leg fractures that had healed. The only way they could have survived such injuries was if other members of a pack had brought them food.

SNAPPING JAWS

HYAENODON

Feel like a nice relaxing day at the beach? A little sunbathing, swimming, and—er . . . escaping from a *Hyaenodon*! This creature was one of the first big carnivorous mammals. It had massive jaws supported by extra muscles in its neck—and it used them to crush animal skulls. We know this because a fossil of an early type of cat called *Dinictis* has holes in its skull that match the tooth pattern of *Hyaenodon*. What's more, fossilized *Hyaenodon* waste contains pieces of animal skull.

Hyaenodon did not rely just on crushing animals in its jaws. It also had slicing teeth at the back of these jaws. As the animal grew older, these slicing teeth would grind against each other, keeping them sharp. As a result, it could eat smaller pieces rather than gulping down large chunks, which would help with digestion. To avoid being chewed up into very small pieces, these beachgoers need to get up that lifeguard tower. It's a very appropriately named tower, if you think about it.

HYAENODON

PRONOUNCED
Hi-EE-noh-don

LIVED
Plains of North America, Europe, Asia, and Africa, 40 million–20 million years ago

LENGTH
Just over 10 feet (3 m) (the largest species, *Hyaenodon gigas*)

RIVAL PREDATORS

Why did *Hyaenodon* die out? It might have had competition from "bear dogs," such as *Amphicyon.* These were as lethal as *Hyaenodon* but probably faster, so they were better able to catch scurrying herbivores.

TIMELINE

DIMETRODON

Named after the Greek for "two measures of teeth"

Dimetrodons had incisors for gripping, stabbing canines, curved rear teeth for shearing flesh, and teeth in the roof of the mouth to pin down prey.

SARCOSUCHUS

Named after the Greek for "flesh crocodile"

Sarcosuchus' long snout had a bowl-shaped ending called a bulla. Scientists are not sure what it was for. It may have helped the crocodile to smell or allowed it to make calls to fellow *Sarcosuchus*.

QUETZALCOATLUS

Named after the Aztec flying serpent god, Quetzalcoatl

Most scientists think *Quetzalcoatlus* ate small animals on land as a modern stork does. But others think it scavenged dead carcasses like a vulture or skimmed up fish in its long beak like a seabird.

INOSTRANCEVIA

Named after Russian geologist Alexandr Inostrantzev

The herbivore *Scutosaurus* was probably one of *Inostrancevia*'s main meals. It was massively built and heavily armored but could not have outrun *Inostrancevia*.

PHORUSRHACID

Named after the Greek for "bearing wrinkles or scars"

The lands of North and South America joined about 3 million years ago, and at least one species of terror bird, the *Titanis*, migrated to North America. Its remains have been found in Texas and Florida.

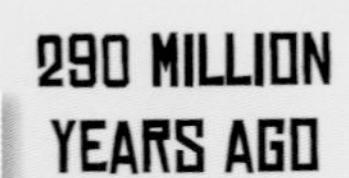

290 MILLION YEARS AGO

Around 230 million years ago: First dinosaurs evolve

66 million years ago: End of the dinosaurs

HYAENODON

Named after the Greek for "hyena tooth"

Hyaenodon microdon, the smallest species of *Hyaenodon*, was not a massive wolf-sized creature—it was only about the size of a house cat.

ANDREWSARCHUS

Named after naturalist Roy Chapman Andrews and the Greek *archos*, for "ruler"

Andrewsarchus is widely considered to be the largest carnivorous land mammal ever. Today's largest is the polar bear.

SMILODON

Named after the Greek for "knife/saber tooth"

Saber-toothed cats evolved from the Carnivora group of mammals about 42 million years ago. Their acute senses made them excellent hunters. *Smilodon* was one of the last saber-toothed cats.

AMBULOCETUS

Named after the Latin *ambulare* (to walk) and *cetus* (whale)

Chemical analysis of *Ambulocetus*' teeth shows it lived in fresh and salt water. Maybe it lived in river estuaries where fresh water meets the sea—or it went anywhere to find a meal.

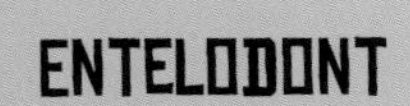

ENTELODONT

Named after the Greek for "perfect tooth"

Entelodonts were probably omnivores and also apex predators in North America, Europe, and Asia. *Andrewsarchus* was closely related to Entelodonts.

50 MILLION YEARS AGO

10,000 YEARS AGO

UNCOVERING THE PAST

Scientists reconstruct prehistoric beasts from their fossilized body parts, which helps them understand how the animals lived. One of the best-known dinosaur finds is, of course, the top predator *Tyrannosaurus rex* (*right*)—and one of the few complete skeletons of *T. rex* is in the American Museum of Natural History in New York City.

The displays in museums are not made from real fossil bones. These are fragile and precious and must be carefully stored away. Instead museum staff make lightweight replicas of fossils and use these to construct skeletons, often covering them with synthetic skin, scales, or fur.

Mythical Fossils

Paleontology, or the study of fossils, has come far since early times. There are people who link tales about mythical creatures such as the griffin (a mixture of lion and eagle) to the discovery of dinosaur fossils. There is little evidence for this, but it is true that early fossil finds seemed very puzzling. In 1676 a British professor named Robert Plot was given a fossil of an unusually large thigh bone. When describing it, he said it must have come from a giant race of humans! In fact, it was from a *Megalosaurus* dinosaur.

Reconstructing Skeletons

When scientists are exceptionally lucky, they find complete skeletons of animals to work from. But usually there are missing bones.The bones may have broken up while the animal was being buried. Sometimes a predator ate some bones of the animal it killed!

However, scientists can remake the whole animal by comparing its skeleton with other skeletons of the same animal. They often know where the muscles were positioned because the bones sometimes have scars where the muscles were attached. Once they have an idea of the size of the muscles, they can estimate the animal's weight.

What the skin was like is a different matter. Occasionally when an animal is buried in fine soil that hardens quickly, it is preserved—but usually it isn't! So scientists often disagree about the skin of prehistoric animals, arguing over its color and texture and whether it had fur or feathers.

INDEX

The Author

Matthew Rake lives in London, in the United Kingdom, and has worked in publishing for more than twenty years. He has written on a wide variety of topics for adults as well as children, including science, sports, and the arts.

The Illustrator

Award-winning illustrator Simon Mendez combines his love of nature and drawing by working as an illustrator with a focus on scientific and natural subjects. He paints on a wide variety of themes but mainly concentrates on portraits and animal subjects. He lives in the United Kingdom.